WS

Materials

Comparing Materials

Cassie Mayer

Heinemann LIBRARY

H www.heinemannlibrary.co.uk
Visit our website to find out more information about Heinemann Library books.

To order:
☎ Phone 44 (0) 1865 888066
🖹 Send a fax to 44 (0) 1865 314091
💻 Visit the Heinemann Bookshop at www.heinemannlibrary.co.uk to browse our catalogue and order online.

Heinemann Library is an imprint of Pearson Education Limited, a company incorporated in England and Wales having its registered office at Edinburgh Gate, Harlow, Essex, CM20 2JE – Registered company number: 00872828

Heinemann is a registered trademark of Pearson Education Limited.

Text © Pearson Education Limited 2009
First published in hardback in 2009
The moral rights of the proprietor have been asserted.

Edited by Rebecca Rissman and Sian Smith
Designed by Kimberley R. Miracle and Joanna Hinton-Malivoire
Picture research by Tracy Cummins and Tracey Engel
Production by Duncan Gilbert
Originated by Dot
Printed and bound in China by Leo Paper Group

ISBN 978 0 43119301 4
13 12 11 10 09
10 9 8 7 6 5 4 3 2 1

British Library Cataloguing in Publication Data

Mayer, Cassie
    Comparing materials. - (Acorn plus)
    1. Materials science - Juvenile literature
    620.1'1

A full catalogue record for this book is available from the British Library.

Acknowledgements
We would like to thank the following for permission to reproduce photographs: ©Agefotostock **p. 10** (Targa); ©AP Photo **p. 22** Bottom Right (Kai-Uwe Knoth); ©CORBIS **pp. 4** Bottom Left (Perry Mastrovito), **12** Left (Keystone/Martin Ruetschi), **14** Right (Lowell Georgia); ©Getty Images **pp. 12** Right (Yuka Kisugi), **16** Right (George Diebold); ©Heinemann Raintree **pp. 5 Top** Left, **8**, **17** Right, **20** Left, **21** Left, **21** Right, **22** Top Right (David Rigg); ©iStockphoto **pp. 17** Left (johanna goodyear), **22** Bottom Left (Mikael Damkier); ©photos.com **p. 9** Right (Jupiter Images); ©Shutterstock **4** Bottom Right (Rick Seeney), **4** Top Left (Polina Lobanova), **4** Top Right (Aron Brand), **5** Bottom Left (Anette Linnea Rasmussen), **5** Bottom Right (TomTom), **5** Top Left (Anastasiya Igolkina), **6** (Bob Hosea), **7** (Vova Pomortzeff), **9** Left (Holly Kuchera), **11** (Yanta), **18** (EcoPrint), **19** (dpaint), **13** Left (Mike Norton), **13** Right (Johnny Lye), **14** Left (prism_68), **15** Left (Marco Rametta), **15** Right (Wendy Kaveney Photography), **16** Left (Timura), **20** Right (Can Balcioglu), **21** Middle (freelanceartist), **22** Top Left (Wally Stemberger).

Cover photographs reproduced with permission of ©iStockphoto glass (David Wilkins); ©Shutterstock metal (Ronald Sumners), plastic (Kheng Guan Toh), rocks (Anastasiya Igolkina), rubber (Roman Sigaev), soil (Luminis), water (anbk), wood (Ozger Aybike Sarikaya).

Back cover photographs reproduced with permission ©Corbis/Perry Mastrovito (plastic) and ©Shutterstock/Anette Linnea Rasmussen (metal).

The publishers would like to thank Nancy Harris for her assistance in the preparation of this book.

Every effort has been made to contact copyright holders of material reproduced in this book. Any omissions will be rectified in subsequent printings if notice is given to the publishers.

Contents

Some words appear in bold, **like this**. You can find out what they mean in "Words to know" on page 23.

Let's look at materials

wood

water

plastic

rubber

We can use materials to make different things. Some materials come from nature, such as wood and water. Some materials are made by people, such as plastic and rubber.

glass

rocks

metal

soil

Materials have different **properties**. They can be different sizes, shapes, and colours. They can be rough or smooth. They can be heavy or light. They can be stiff or **flexible**.

Let's compare wood and metal

Wood is a natural material that comes from trees. Wood is changed by water. Wood will **rot** if it is left in water for a long time. It gets weak and breaks into pieces.

Metal is a natural material that comes from rocks. Some metals are changed by water. They **rust** if they are left in water for a long time. They get weak and turn reddish-brown.

Wood is changed by fire. It burns and turns to ash.

Metal is changed by very hot fire. It changes into a **liquid**. Liquids do not have a shape. Then metal cools and hardens into a new shape.

Let's compare glass and rocks

Glass is a **man-made** material. Glass is made from sand. The sand is mixed with other **ingredients**. The mixture is then melted to make glass. Glass is a strong material, but it can break.

Rocks are natural materials. They are found in nature. Rocks are very strong.

Some rocks are very big. Some rocks are as small as a grain of sand.

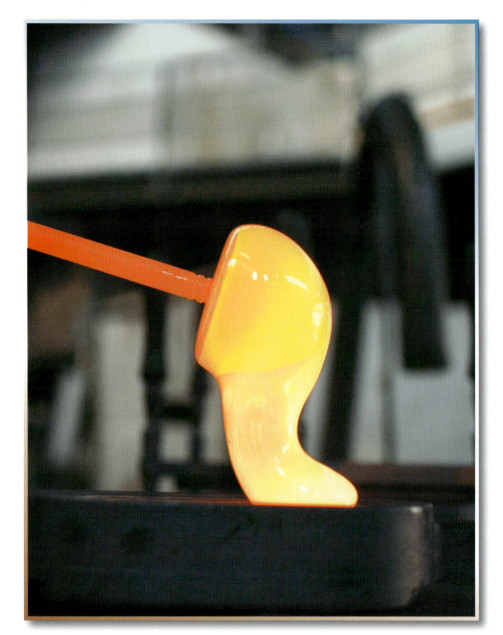

Glass changes at a very high heat. It melts into a **liquid**. Liquids do not have a shape. Then glass cools and hardens into a new shape.

Rocks change over time. Wind and water **erode** rocks. Wind and water wear rocks away.

Let's compare plastic and rubber

oil

Plastic is a **man-made** material that is made from oil.
The oil is mixed with other **ingredients** to make plastic.

sap

Most rubber is a man-made material that is made from oil. The oil is mixed with other ingredients to make rubber. Some rubber is made from the **sap** of a rubber tree.

Some plastic is strong and cannot bend. Some plastic is **flexible**. It can bend backwards and forwards.

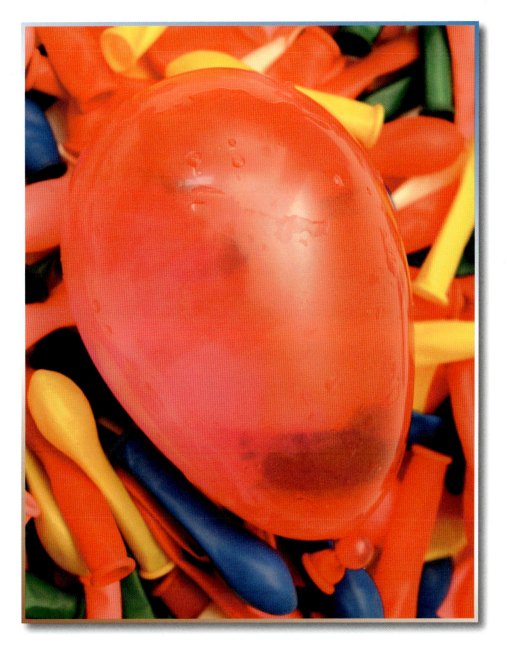
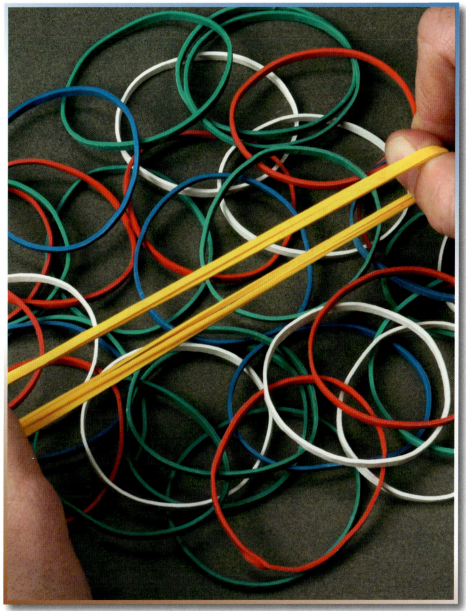

Rubber can be flexible. Rubber can bend backwards and forwards. Rubber can be soft. It can also stretch.

Let's compare water and soil

Water is a natural material. Water falls from clouds as rain, ice, and snow. All plants and animals need water.

Soil is a natural material. Soil covers the Earth. It is made of tiny rocks and dead plants. Plants need soil.

Water can change form. It freezes when it is very cold. It becomes a **solid**. A solid is something that has a shape.

Water boils when it gets very hot. It becomes a **gas**. A gas is a substance in the air that has no shape.

peat

clay

sand

Soil can be made of different things. Peat soil is found in wet areas and has lots of dead plants in it. Clay is found near rocks and has lots of **minerals** in it. Sandy soil is made mostly of tiny rocks or shells.

How do we use materials?

All materials have different **properties** that make them useful. We use materials to make new things. We use materials every day.

Words to know

erode	wear away over time
flexible	can bend backwards and forwards
gas	substance in the air that has no shape
man-made	made by people
ingredient	something that is added to make something new
liquid	flowing substance that has no shape
minerals	things that are found in rocks
porous	lets in liquids and gases
property	certain feature of an object, such as its shape or colour
rot	break down over time
rust	to be weakened by water; when metal rusts, it turns reddish-brown
sap	the runny, sticky part of a plant
solid	something that has a shape
transparent	see-through

Index

Note to parents and teachers

Before reading

Explain to children that we use the word *material* to describe something that takes up space and can be used to make other things. Then, help students make a list of different types of materials.

After reading

Turn to page 22 and ask children to identify the materials shown in each of the thumbnail photos.

Ask children to choose two materials from pages 4 and 5 and make a Venn diagram comparing their properties. Explain to the children that the intersection of the two circles should show properties that the materials have in common.